For Marty and Tania —

The Lost Poems of Cangjie

with warm wishes on your anniversary —

John and Carol —
April 28, 2017

Seventeenth-century portrait of Cangjie (detail) by an unknown artist.

The Lost Poems of Cangjie

THE XIAN SCROLLS

The Poems of Cangjie *with* Visions of Cangjie

Translations and Afterword by E. O.
Foreword by John Briscoe

Published by RiskPress
825 Gravenstein Highway North, Suite 12
Sebastopol, California 95472
pkcp@aol.com

Copyright © John Briscoe, 2016

ISBN: 978-0-9848403-4-2

Without limiting the rights under copyright reserved above, no part of this publication (except in the case of brief quotations embodied in critical articles or reviews) may be reproduced, stored in, or introduced into a retrieval system or transmitted in any format or by any means (electronic, mechanical, photocopying, recording, or otherwise) without the express written permission of both the copyright holder and the above publisher of this book. The scanning, uploading, and distribution of this book via the Internet or via any other means without the permission of the publisher is illegal and punishable by law. Please purchase only authorized electronic editions and do not participate in or encourage electronic piracy of copyrightable materials. Your support of the author's rights is appreciated.

Front (detail) and back (full artwork) covers: *Winter Blossom*, 2011, by Hung Liu. Woodcut with acrylic; 23.25 x 23.5 in. Copyright © 2011 by Hung Liu, reproduced courtesy of the artist.

Printed in China by Global PSD.

10 9 8 7 6 5 4 3 2 1
FIRST EDITION

Contents

Foreword   *John Briscoe*   ix

The Xian Scrolls

   The Beta Scroll: Visions of Cangjie   3

   The Alpha Scroll: The Poems of Cangjie   13

Afterword: Finding Cangjie   *E. O.*   63

Foreword

This book presents the first translations, into any language, of the poetry of Cangjie, historian in the court of China's Yellow Emperor who reigned, according to tradition, for a hundred years, from 2697 to 2597 BCE. Though Cangjie is a well-known figure even today in Chinese history, and legend, and though he was almost certainly a poet, neither history nor legend mentions his poetry. How his poems came to be preserved, and how the preserved poems came to be discovered, is explained in the afterword by E.O. In brief, a sculptor working in the tile kilns and factories of the First Emperor, the emperor who ordered the building of the underground Terra-Cotta Army 2400 years after Cangjie lived, transcribed the poems onto a scroll. "Translated" may be more accurate. The Sculptor, as E.O. names him, was himself a poet, who composed a number of poems around this time, which he rendered on a second scroll. The sculptor secreted both scrolls well; they were discovered only a few decades ago. The Alpha Scroll contains the poems of Cangjie as written out by the Sculptor. As E.O. explains in his afterword, these poems now stand as the oldest known poetry on earth. The Beta Scroll contains the Sculptor's own poems.

How I, a lawyer whose practice takes me to East Asia, came to meet E.O., and in time be asked to act as agent to bring this work to publication, is a story both convoluted and confidential, but at all events unnecessary to this book. This assignment has been a singularly gratifying privilege. That Charlie Pendergast and Risk Press — whose passion for poetry, typography, and bookmaking is unsurpassed — agreed to produce this book makes it doubly gratifying. In addition to Charlie's generous support of the first edition of this book, E. O. wishes also to acknowledge the invaluable help of Tom Christensen; John Stuckey, library director of the Asian Art Museum of San Francisco; Alev Croutier; Noreen Wong; and Sara Mumolo and Matthew Zapruder of the St. Mary's College of California MFA Program in Creative Writing. Proceeds from the sale of this book will be given to that program's scholarship fund.

I have no qualifications as literary critic, much less of Chinese poetry, but I will offer one small observation on this collection of translations. Until now, the oldest known Chinese poem was "The Peasant's Song," dating from perhaps the twelfth century BCE. That poem contains dismissive contempt for "an emperor."

Later, in the third century BCE, 213 to be precise, the First Emperor ordered the Burning of the Books, an act meant to abolish poetry and learning among the people, and confine it to the emperor and his personal scholars. That event, ironically, led to the preservation of Cangjie's poems, already by that time almost twenty-five hundred years old.

A thousand years after the Burning of the Books the great poet Li Bai was called to the court of the Tang emperor, and among his assignments, as E. O. tells us, was to compose odes to the emperor's favorite concubine. They are stirring, even loving odes. For whatever reason — those odes or other matters — the emperor expelled Li Bai from the court. The poet ever after was "the Banished Immortal."

In the latter years of the twentieth century CE, Mao Zedong crushed art, literature, and learning during the ten-year Cultural Revolution from 1966 until 1976. Now we learn, turning back in time almost five thousand years, that Cangjie composed his poems while serving in the court of the Yellow Emperor, who raged jealous of Cangjie's friendship with, and apparent affection for, the emperor's favorite courtesan. The Yellow Emperor ordered Cangjie never again to speak to her, meaning never again to recite to her his verse. And so Cangjie invented writing, not for the reason the histories have told for almost five thousand years, but for a most personal one — to possess a means to deliver to his beloved, and muse, his poems.

In our day we have a Chinese ruler who seeks, it sometimes seems, to place himself in that pantheon of Chinese rulers dating back almost five thousand years. Cangjie's poems have a bracing, though rueful, relevance today.

John Briscoe
San Francisco, August 2016

The Lost Poems of Cangjie

for 靈魂

"*Poetry is what is lost in translation*"
— *Robert Frost*

The Beta Scroll

Visions of Cangjie

Poems of the Sculptor,
the translator of the Poems of Cangjie
Qin Dynasty, *circa* 213 BCE

White spires,
    or lavender petals
    of wisteria blooms in spring—
or was it eyes he saw in a moon, or a moon
    [—in eyes?—]

No whim, no mere decree
of any emperor
could have conjured
Cangjie's sorcery.

◐

These gouges and etches, these inks
and watercolor washes
should draw not only snow tracks
of herons, droplets
of stilled waves about to break
on rocks, but the mouthed sounds
of speech.
    Painter Cangjie thought this
before the edicts fell.

◐

Had Cangjie not, I
to tell the beauty that hovers
over the moon
and hovers over you,
would have worked in time a way
to scratch in unbaked clay or bone,
or paint in inks on silk
pictures of words
    — I would paint first
     [words, oldest words?]

   ◐

One woman walked
as a falcon in soar.
All painters of the court and country
wanted to paint her.

One odd one,
more poet than painter,
wanted to talk with her
not to talk to her
but to hear her.

   ◐

Hers was the name of a stream
falling,
careening.
Cangjie asked
to walk with her.

☽

Three times Cangjie asked
that she walk with him.
Three times she made no answer.
Nine moons later they met
by a willow stand late in morning
and she nodded.
They walked, stood, walked, and stood.
    Cangjie spoke and spoke
waiting to listen.
    He waited until the Yellow River rose
in spring
    [...].

☽

The emperor watched her walk [ ]
the far bank of the Jiang [the Wei, the Jing, the Yellow?]
and with osprey eyes
saw Cangjie speak to her
his poems,
     the emperor thought.

◐

The emperor summoned Cangjie
to the inner court of the palace
and ordered he devise a means
more effectual than knots in cords and ropes,
than memories of courtiers and callers
to carry imperial decrees across the countryside,
to impress them on the countryside.

◐

The first to be so recorded
was the newest decree:
> Following the first full moon of fall
> Cangjie was not to see nor speak
> to her or [her lady, her retinue?]¹

◐

Cangjie watched
in mudded shallows
the tracks long-legged
wading birds made,
little prints the feet of song birds
left in snow.

◐

---

1   The impulse to annotate can be irresistible, and this is such an occasion. More than three thousand years later than the Yellow Emperor's decree here written of, Li Bai (Li Po) arrived at the capital of Changan (modern Xian). He was appointed to the Hanlin Academy ("the writing brush forest") by Emperor Xuan-zong, or Hsuan Tsung in older English spellings. There he met Du Fu (Tu Fu), the two became life-long friends, and they composed poetry for the enjoyment of the emperor, and the favorite of his three thousand "palace ladies," the beautiful Yang Kuei-fei. Three of the poems to Lady Yang are translated in Shigeyoshi Obata, tr., *The Works of Li Po* (New York: E. P. Dutton & Co., 1922), 31–34. Soon after, Li Bai was expelled from the court and made to leave Changan. That is when a friend named him the "banished immortal." *The Anchor Book of Chinese Poetry*, 117. Had Cangjie suffered, in effect, a similar fate?

This new emperor calls himself
First Emperor.
Why does he not announce himself
the Second Yellow Emperor
Or More Yellow Emperor?
He is no more first
than Yellow Emperor was.

◐

All things written must be made his or burned,
all to make him First.
His soldiers may break and burn the bones and urns
of Cangjie's odes, but his words
wrapped [mummiform?] in these silks
will lie a thousand years beneath
their flailing clubs, their flaming torches.

◐

Over and over I sculpt and paint
    some fierce scowl
        on some frightened warrior —
never a whinnying horse,
never a mincing dancer.
Why can't I build
one winged chariot
to fly me away from here?

◐

Birds skittering, hopping
strutting, swaggering (those crows) —
all make pictures with their feet
that Cangjie saw,
pictures of words.

Prints of shrill birds —
ravens, and [those crows again?] —
were pictures of words
for "foul," for "offal."

The prints of feet of song birds
were pictures of words
for moonset, and breast
and yes.

An egret leapt into flight
leaving in sand the etched word
love.

◐

[indecipherable]

◐

[indec. fragment]

◐

Cangjie and she
stood a last time
below the high bank of the [Wei?] River.
He showed her the tracks of birds,
the method he had made.
She had learned music,
she had learned silk,
and she was the first
    to learn this art,
the furious emperor
would later find.
    Only she would ever know
    the pictures of the words [. . .]
    until he. . . .

◐

Thus was one woman so [ ] Cangjie,
forbidden by the emperor to be with her,
invented writing so she could hold
and read alone aloud to herself
poems of her and her [ ] in her
the moon Cangjie alone could see.

◐

First Emperor is only
an emperor, only
another emperor.
But this emperor burns our books.
Burners of books
in the end burn people.

The Alpha Scroll

The Poems of Cangjie

Circa 2650 BCE

You have listened to my poems. Now
I teach you
to see them   to […]

◐

Moon over the far field,
    round as a Laughing Buddha,
you have no man's eyes
but a woman's,
    serene as hers
    when hers are.[2]

◐

What eyes you have,
    you the moon,
       the serene eyes
       within her eyes.

◐

2   The sculptor, the transcriber of 2200 years ago, must have used "Buddha" as a substitute for a word or simile of Cangjie's that he could not work out. What forgotten god or figure might have been the subject for which "Buddha" was substituted?

More in this poem perplexes. While the historical Buddha had lived three hundred years before the sculptor, his teachings have generally been thought not to have reached China for some considerable time after the era of the First Emperor. But some recent scholarship might suggest otherwise — that not only was Buddhism established during the reign of the First Emperor but it was a sect the emperor sought to suppress, just as he sought to suppress all other learning (except for himself). The *China Daily* for May 13, 2009 (*www.chinadaily.com.cn/life/2009-05/13/content_7772181.htm*), reported:

> The first emperor of a united China could go down in history not only for the Great Wall or the terracotta army of guards and horses, but also for his attempt to crush Buddhism, which was widely prevalent at that time, according to a researcher on Monday.
>
> "China's first and most influential history book, *The Historical Records*, stated clearly that Emperor Qin Shihuang (259–210 BC) strictly banned Buddhism and Buddhist temples," says Han Wei, a noted researcher with the Shaanxi Provincial Institute of Archeology.
>
> According to the *Historical Records*, the ban went alongside the emperor's major military strategies including the deportation of the invading Huns, and was applied far beyond the ancient capital Xianyang in today's Xi'an to cover the whole country. Emperor Qin Shihuang's ban on Buddhism indicated the religion was already popular in China's interior regions in his reign, says Han, whose thesis on the subject was published last week in Xi'an.

Like your lashes
your hands flutter —
quails in a bush
at an approach —
    mine
        this time.

◐

    Your eyes
slow
    to beat in time
        with your heart.

So your eyes have heard their heart —
        — in my poem?

◐

Your hands slow too
    like your eyes
from their lash flutter.
    In time your hands will move in time
        to your eyes, in time
        to theirs.

◐

Dogwood leaves in May sway
light, like your hands
opening to tell,
    spilling petals
        onto my stumbling,
            onto my path.

◐

Emperor is jealous of you your beauty,
what he thinks
    all can see.
If he could see what Cangjie sees,
what even this impudence
won't let me call [. . .],
his rage would rise [ ].
He would kill [ ]

◐

If Emperor could see your true [ ]
awe would banish [. . . his vanity? envy?].

◐

Emperor practices jealousy
as if it were an art
like falconry, or archery.
He more than lusts,
he is more than jealous,
he is envious of the beauty
sleeping languid in your skin
and not in his.
He seethes when he sees you before him.
Does he take you thinking
you will ravish him
and he will be reborn as you?

◐

His are the leathered blotches and warts
of a swine his age.
Draped in his hide,
you must wallow in his mire —
don't let it sully you.

◐

Jealousy has made mad
the emperor.
How more mad would he be
    if he could see you?

◐

Emperor would rather be
than have you
and does not know.

◐

The court lights — has a sun pierced
　　clouds outside?
　　　　No, it is you entering,
　　　　　　smiling. You have, I think,
　　　　　　　drunk more than a cup of wine.

◐

A band of players pipes
　　a tune, an air —
no, it is you
　　laughing
　　　somewhere in the open court.
I will have another cup
brought to you.

◐

Green snow peas
    shelled,
a fistful of little
    white onions,
are beads of jade
    and pearls strung
and tossed in a bowl the color
    the alabaster of your throat.

◐

A drop of dew
from the dimple
where the stem holds the fruit
slides slow down the blushed face
of the peach I want —
    a tear
    from your eye.

◐

A fish jumped near
the clump of willows
at the river's bank,
or an osprey or egret
    speared a fish.
You saw the commotion and ran to it and I,
I saw you are a dancer.

◐

Too far to see I want to ask,
Did the fish or egret
pause for you too?

    ◐

    Where does Lei Zu take you
mornings after the loom?
To the emperor's bedchamber
I know.

You do not walk then
    as a dancer walks,
        nor after.

    ◐

Do you dance for him?
Do you bare for Emperor
your lithe ivory limbs?

I wished to be emperor once
to see that dance.
But I would rather now
hear your heart,
to listen to its dance.

    ◐

Summer — you wear chemises
with shorter sleeves.

The light from your wrists —
is it the sun mirrored,
or the opaque light
in you?

◐

Black cod, baked,
white rice and bok choy
dressed with onion shoots,
if she, your cook, would tire,
I would cook for you
an autumn afternoon
in rain.

◐

Black cod, butterfish, sablefish —
many Huang He [many Yellow River ?]
— too many names
for one fish.

Whatever its name
I will learn it well
so you will want me
to be your cook.

◐

Who will I walk with
if not you?
I will walk
with no one,
not even me.

◐

Where water runs through rocks you stand
shutting your eyes
to listen. What you hear
is not what I hear.
I grieve
     as at death.

◐

Your hand
brushed my hand
hours ago.
Was it
inadvertent?

Now the moon rises
and with it my hand
heavenward.

◐

You looked at me
long, I thought.

I saw there

a long white valley
behind the moon.

◐

Lover I have not loved,
your sweetened griefs asleep beneath
heavy arms of the emperor,
my gaze in waft,
blood ebbing
from my hands and face

I sit by window-racing moon
while about the night sweet griefs
sing in sway-sleep chorus
and dream unuttered words of age —
Before the moon was called
to its wind-kept flight
were we not known,
Lover I have not loved?

◐

The rising moon
torments.
The wide horizon of world
falls farther, farther from it
as it winks
and taunts.

◐

Why do I look to the face of the moon?
Your face isn't here:
Such
an idle answer.

◐

What face hovered
when I was born?
It was the moon's,
or yours.

It was the moon's.

It was yours.

◐

You the moon, I
am an idle star —
all I do is turn
slow whorls
around you.

◐

You are older than you think and I
 much younger.

Old knowledge wells in you,
young folly
 in me.

◐

(He ascends a Canyon)

Beyond where others stop because
they find their passage blocked
I walk on and find a pool
fed by a waterfall
    almost all the year.

I thought to find an ancestor there,
perhaps the shade of my father,
but in the pool I see the glimmer
of your inner manner,
clear water
over gleaming stones.

   ☽

(within the canyon)

One leaf among ten thousand
twirls in these trees
in an unfelt breeze —
    a pinwheel spun
  by an unseen finger.

Ten thousand words to you have [burned — ?]

   ☽

How can dabs and idle slashes
    in clay,
when fired foreordained
    to be smashed to shards,
fly your heart like a phoenix
    to my odd wood to be born?

◐

Where below the pool
below the waterfall
the stream fall steepens
the water roils in the rocks
and drops beneath gnarls
of overhanging limbs of trees
sounding a pealing — sounding
    ling.

Downstream the creek turns
abrupt toward the sea,
and rushes
    a long *won*.

Ling won is the name
of the water that hurtles boulders,
that careens around
one last long bend
on its sad-song way to the sea.

◐

Hidden in hillsides of the north,
I am a pool. Waters seeping
from the rocks and castled crags
are your words I cannot hear
keeping me at brim.

◐

Women spinning silk,
    weaving on their looms,
men playing war with sticks
    and doing calisthenics —.
Why do I write of these
    and cherry trees —
      their blooming, and leafing, and fruiting —
        when what I am thinking is you?

◐

The *si* and *gong*
[of right and wrong? —]
    were it so simple.

  ◐

Why do I look with such longing at the moon
this hour before dawn so clear
the air itself blown away
by last night's storm?
    Those are not eyes, I know,
   but are eyes I have known
though I cannot remember when,
nor when I had first seen yours
a million years ago.

  ◐

Moon over the ridge of night,
eyes gaunt, and hollow,
your mouth cries —
    are you parched,
    are you cold?

  ◐

Moon beneath
wide Huang He —
What have you to do
with the moon above you?

☽

Skies gray with rain
cannot clear before
fogs rise
from last year's rice fields.
All winter there is no moon to ask
    for one more spring.

☽

Were it for me I would see
these cherry trees
bloom once more, and wake to pick
a basket of black-red cherries
and a poem of yellow cherries
from the stout word-tree of summer
drooping with fruit —
these I would [. . . ?].

☽

Moon,
you moan —
I see but cannot
hear you.
What is it
you strain to say?

☽

Cod thrash
the boat bottom.

Throes ceased, their eyes
are lotus blossoms.

☽

I know you only little
but know you as I know
my heart pulled
as the sea by the moon
may seem to be.

☽

Moon, you rise
far east of east
so large and red
you frighten first —
a glower
from Emperor.

Night rises and you pale.
Your eyes sadden, ashen
and shrink. I see now
you are alone as I,
but without this wine
to drink.

☽

A slip of moon
hangs in the west,
awaiting word.
But I and my me
we are occupied
drinking never again
to piety,
but to pity.

☽

Willows on river banks,
pines on hills
are best for hiding nights
from the blare of days.

Calls of animals, strange,
assure. Surely
we knew once; surely
they're not us,
but better.

    ◐

So close, and afire
    at nightrise,
at midnight, moon,
    you are cold
        and afar.

I will await you again in morning
when you will come close again
and then descend
beyond the western desert,
behind the Bayan Har.

    ◐

You once asked I pick
one persimmon for you.
Ask me again please
when there is a moon
and stars fall
hard as hail.

◐

Night stills, my small room
stills. I sleep.
A breeze
washes my cheeks
and eyes like water
as if I were floating
beneath a river's ripples.

I stir myself awake
but no breeze stirs
Air and my room
are frozen as ground.
The breeze was only time
flowing, ebbing
to its Bohai Sea.

◐

Your sandal chafes.
You stop to sit on the stoop of the boathouse
to remove it, looking
    at the far bank
       where nothing is,
       where nothing moves,
idly rubbing your foot.

You are his chosen [sweet?]
but he ill provides for you.
I would happily be
made minder of your feet.

◐

Your chestnut eyes, nearly still,
follow the darting flight
    of a bird I cannot see.

    Bird
      and eyes
        madden me.

◐

Our eyes have not met
for a month
      a year.
Do yours no longer feel
 the pull of mine?

◐

Moon, I pine for you.
Were you once
      not this indifferent?

◐

The moon rises unblinking--
indifferent as you.

◐

Shimmering flame ball,
the moon lifts late
a glower in fall
in the east.

[. . .] in the cold, cold east . . . .

◐

Day dies,
night rises —
welcome purple shroud.
Why do I think I may find you
underneath?

☽

I am singing to you
soft.
I am singing I am
speaking to you
with quirking brush this
long late night so
moonless I cannot see
so soft I cannot hear
its zags and whorls brushed
on these plaited silken pages
where unseeing and unhearing
I write you straining
to hear you.[3]

☽

---

[3] Though the sculptor, the transcriber of Cangjie's poems, reports he rendered them onto silk from the bones and pottery on which he had found them carved, Cangjie was a painter, and silk fabric, according at least to legend, was invented in his time. Still, the sculptor may have taken license here, and substituted "silken pages" for whatever Cangjie's poem described as its medium.

Remembrances of young times are dim,
    but I recall thinking once
that a music of melodic words,
a desolate thunder pounding as drums,
could quicken a dead heart,
and fly it like a phoenix
to a dying heart.

◐

Why I, imprisoned,
write my madness —
So you may know the depths and heights
your heart can sound
and soar.

◐

Do you dance for him or you?
On your feet you move
like a calling bird,
not one on foot,
in flight.

◐

Day always has
> its sunrise
> seen or not.
Night sometimes misses moonrise,
> even the slenderest shaving
> of a shadow of the faded moon —
>> What grief then wracks

our night's black shroud?

◐

You alone of ladies
wear no flowers.
You are kind not to dim
a lotus blossom.

◐

What alabaster ornament
would not pale at your nape, or throat?
What jade or ruby would not fade
at your cheek?
What lotus bud dares bloom
in the moonrise of your eyes?

◐

Were I to hear you, you would hear
the serene song, see
the far pools
of the long horizon of your soul.
I would hear little of what you would hear
and see again —
first moonrise.

◐

I must not speak your name
nor now that I have made
drawings of names
draw it.

◐

靈魂 first
were pictures etched
    of the sounds of soul,
then of the sounds
    of the name of soul,
      then of soul.

靈魂 too
are painted pictures of the sounds of you,
of the sounds of the name of you,
    of your name
      looming.

Silk words for soul, silk words for you
    are *ling won*. You
      are *ling won*.

◐

Archer in the army of the emperor,
I exchanged my quiver
for a sheath of words.

My aim remained the heart
though never did it err
as now.

◐

I, inventor of writing,
had I had my choice
would be instead inventor
of words
    — or finder, rather.
Words were always there,
though hidden, bidden
to be found, in the sound
of a creek, of rain on a roof,

of the hiss of silence.
What of the ones not found yet?
What strange, rich things
they must speak of.

◐

Red goji berries,
yellow cherries
picked bright
vie for the ravishing
of wine.

◐

    Hoarfrost — an aureole rings the moon.
She surely is as cold as I.

…

    Wide sky without horizon —
clouds array in rows as far
as horizon would be,
like ranks of Emperor's archers,
columns of his chariots.

…

Forty swords upraised is this
odd bush, as from one hilt, though only one
stirs, waving now, now brandishing
wildly tilting at the sky
while the others
stand still.

...

No dream is stranger than
this world that is all
I know.

◐

Blue lupine, poppies
opened gold in spring in canyons
west of the last rise to the sea
are winter waves battering
rocks below the sea house, are you
sitting at a window there,
watching rain thinking
of baking,
of a poem of baking,
of me writing
this.

◐

Sing of song and idleness
for love is not for having.
The hours I sing of trifling
are all there is in living.

I idle in wine, addle in words,
and imagine you keep mine to say
aloud by dimmest lamplight
till comes the rapping on your bedside door

summoning you
to Emperor's bed-chamber.

◐

Listen to the red-pated
male bird sing
to the lady on the farthest limb,
who fluffs her wings and sings herself
made wild as a mad woman.

Words are our poor
birdsong, poorer
than any birdsong.

    O were our words
    pure as the birdsong
    they were.

◐

A tatter of cloud
taunts its cold rage —
The moon is as alone as I.

☽

Words are our
poor birdsong.
The one worth only
of words
is to coax song from you,
 wild rising soaring words.

☽

All words so far found
[are without worth — ?]

☽

Tomorrow, your day,
the moon will have been full
a full day, and just begun to die.
At midnight see the star nearby —
a star of Quail Fire, Willow, or Dipper.
The moon, though,
this night
is I.

☽

New bird in these trees
just beyond the curtained window —
your morning song falters.
Your pacing halts,
your off notes you sing over,
your false notes
you repeat.

She hears.
She sings
aloof and clear
from her higher willow perch
that arches the river.

New bird,
your morning song falters,
like mine.

☽

My heart has flown
    to wait with the moon
      for one who too
    never comes.

☽

Word of your song
     reaches the painters.
They are indifferent to it.
How can they,
     knowing of it,
keep at their painting?

◐

My heart lies with the moon
more alone now
than me.

◐

I see the moon in only you, in none
of the other ladies of the court,
and dancers,
who give such sidelong smiles and glances
that I would be a cheered but tired man
if in one such moon-shaped face I saw
the moon. Sometimes to see
I blindly stare
but it is never there.

◐

Making poems to you
    is a stream in fall
falling,
      caroming off a canyon wall
         stilling to flow slow
      where no wind ripples,
    is hearing
a poem from you.

◐

A poem to you is a river
rushing toward another
larger river
that joins, and pools, and flows
to a sea somewhere
far beyond Bahai

◐

This warmest day
you bare your ivory arms.
Like him others lust them
their most close embrace.

My lust though
is another touch —
your heart alighting
in long unending words
on my barren ears.

◐

No impasto mars
these thin pine planks I hewed,
these silk squares you weaved.
Knives and brushes and color pots
lie in an idle spider's corner.

You cannot sit for me and so
I cannot paint you, so must write you.
If I may see your eyes
one last time
I will write you for ages.

◐

High falls
are the head of this canyon,
the last cascade
from above the highest ridge and trees
that form the horizon overhead.

Where the last chute plunges, the pool
churns, but feet away,
nearer its sill where
it becomes a stream,
it's still
or seems so
and the tranquil water vanishes
and its bottom seems without bottom,
and in it trees and jonquils
and scudding clouds and brooding skies
appear.

This time of year, at midnight,
a full moon peers from under it,
loving, bemused, indifferent.
Would you, if you were here,
see your soul too?

◐

Many springs have passed,
many snows.
I fear I'll be unhearing
before I ever hear you.

◐

Where went his century of reign?
Dead, *he* cannot spear my ears to deafen me.
But his sullen men walk the streets still, stalking.
When they strike may they cut off only
my tongue, and not my hand.

◐

Time moves now
not as in old days when it flowed
languid as the Wei in late summer,
but like the river in torrent spring,
as if it were the emperor's chariot
fitted with a falcon's wings.
Let us walk again. It is early spring.
It is later than we think.

◐

I cannot hear, can scarcely see.
Who are you standing
over me?
You are speaking, that I see.
Whatever are you saying?[4]

◐

Dawn's embers die.
The wide sky ashens,
moans from far
over hills, and weeps —
The morning moon is lost.

◐

Emperor passes —
        dangerous.

Empress passes —
        murderous.

◐

---

4   Cf. Du Fu, "Gone Deaf," eighth century CE:

>Grown old as Ho Kuan Tzu, a hermit
>Lamenting this world, like Lu P'I Weng,
>How long before my sight also dims away?
>For over a month now, deaf as dragons…

>David Hinton, translator, *The Selected Poems of Tu Fu* (New York: New Directions Books, 1988, 97.
>Tony Barnstone and Chou Ping, eds., *The Anchor Book of Chinese Poetry*. New York: Anchor Books 2005), 116
>See generally, http://usa.chinadaily.com.cn/life/2014-12/09/content_19053767.htm.

The Folly of Falling

Like mine for
the weeping moon
mine for the soul I see
beneath your cherry-petal brow
and mouth,
behind your almond eyes
wrings, wracks me too at times
though neither is worth
a sneer or simper,
not even a glance askance
unless it is said so well, so
blithe
that a thousand days from now
children still will laugh aloud
at the silly man
I let me be.

◐

Sly slip
of moon,
you made me wait the night
to see you.
        You
rise in time to greet
my late returning
        shadow.

Now we three shall drink
while we may.

But pink fingers streak the old sky.
Alas, not even the company of you,
my most close of friends,
makes wine taste at dawn.

◐

       Wish —
Time and a while,
 you to listen to, you
     to listen
         to you.

◐

Sun yawns low,
         and red, and rises.
After-winter grasses
        rise and wave —
gold robes and dresses,
         black and chestnut tresses
swaying in breezes fanned
    by your unseen arms
     and [—] dancer's legs.

◐

I would give all life to see
    your arms.
        (Were I to see though
          I would die.)

◐

This cursed collection of words that is
language — dreary, dry, desperate.
Why is there not one that speaks
the pain of that one glimpse
of your wrist?

◐

In winds in falling water,
in scurryings in trees I strain
to hear the lost words of Li Won
poet of uncounted years ago
whose words would make his hearers
bare their breasts to him
[to suckle?].

◐

Li Won's songs, lost for ages,
are lost for ages.
After his life the crippled king
banished those who knew his words
west to the deserts of beasts
of twisted horn and fang
of dreams.

◐

Li Won told of hearing
from a woman of long age
the three first poems.
They were songs of birds,
one white, one red, one gold
who came to her at night.
Their songs were so sweet and sad
no one else could bear to hear them
until the woman heard and learned
and sang them smiling
the first smile.

◐

Today Mother died.
A man from the village of childhood
traveled till dark to bring word
so that I rejoice as the old women
say I must.
                But my eyes are skies
in January rains. My heart trembles
as the bowels of earth can tremble.

What do the wise women know?
The only wisdom
 is there is no wisdom
 including this.

     ◐

Night's hand
lay on my left shoulder light
as I walked the river's bank last evening
hoping to weep at loss of what
was never, hoping to weep at loss
of longing.

Its face I had glimpsed
early in the day
behind my left ear. It did not
expect me so I smiled.
How does a monster of dreams
become a coveted lover?

◐

Long I long
and wish.
     Some writ ought
to banish wish.
Only Emperor ought to wish —
only his wishes
arrive. To long, though,
is the lot of us,
is the resistance
to the pull of the peasant
to the grave.

◐

An old word, long out of use or banned,
no one knows — and no one knows
that no one knows but me,
once-honored historian Cangjie,
I dare write only now:

As the first spring sun loves
damp fields of earth, loves
plains of rivers, plains of eyes,
as the moon loves night and its far eyes,
and loves the eyes of our eyes,
so I too.

◐

No breeze blows, no moonlight
seeps or flows
through black-lit night.
Yet a candle flickers, dims
and dies — how apt
once silly sayings are.

I have written in my years what I could
but much more lies
in any dawn or running stream,
willow bank or osprey flight
or breast burst
at spear point.

Most lies though
in the eyes of the moon —
so near aflame at rise,
so far at zenith, and cold,
so dim or bright, coy
or eager or gone. You

are the moon
creeping in my room years
of sleepless dusks, drunken sleeps,
    fitful midnights dancing
    in every frantic dream
       you chose.

I will cheat the emperor's men.
They will arrive too late for me.
Old, craven, I
    dare write you only now—
        I love you,
           love you as the moon.

    As I write I hear you speak
in no words that I know, poems
never sung before, yours
of a thousand years ago you say
that have no rivers, spears or hours,
    only a music of faintest stars,
    only a faint music of stars.

Afterword: Finding Cangjie

When words first pealed the ecstasy of sunrise, cried the ache of moonrise, sounded the desolation of this life, we don't know. We don't know when sounds first stood as words for *we*, for *home*. We don't know whether a word for *home* existed before a word for returning home, or for the unutterable ache to return home. We do know, though, that like many words, like whole languages, those clusters of words we call poetry arc like meteors. They blaze brief, if at all. If it is particularly right, for its time, or all time, and if the people who spoke it are not all dead or, if written down, and the libraries holding it have not been put to the torch, then a poetry might persist longer, more like a comet than a meteor, a comet plying the night sky that in the end fades into the cosmos. A poetry that survives centuries, however, much less millennia, stands in the firmament like a constellation, wandering at seasons beyond the horizon, but in time returning to the night sky.

◐

Drought parched the Wei River valley, upstream of that river's confluence with the Yellow River, in northern central China the winter of 1974. Late that winter, in mid-March, nine local farmers set out to dig a well east of the city of Xian, twenty kilometers southeast of Xianyang, an ancient capital of China, the capital of the First Emperor and of his short-lived Qin Dynasty. (Twelve centuries before my visit, Xian was called Chang-an, and was the capital of the Tang dynasty during the golden age of Chinese poetry.[1]) One of the farmers, Yang Zhifa clanged his hoe against an object he then exposed, thinking it an earthen jar. It was not a mere jar, but a fragment of a sculpted head, of a life-sized clay warrior. That warrior, it turned out during years of painstaking archaeological digs that followed, was but one of an army of 8000 or more such terra-cotta warriors that had been formed, sculpted, fired, and then buried there, more than two thousand years before.[2]

Chariots and horses in the hundreds were among the army units unearthed in addition to the warriors, charioteers, and archers. Government officials attended the soldiers, as well as factotums wearing belts holstering the tools of the scribe — sleekers (polishers) and knives to smooth and scrape wood, bamboo slats (less precious than silk for writing ordinary words, like those of decrees) — and slinging indispensable whetstones. Accompanying the warriors were acrobats, strongmen and other entertainers. These figures, Chinese scholars have learned, were built in the First Emperor's terra-cotta kilns and manufactories, which had stood nearby. The Wei River valley was the site of early and elaborate drainage and irrigation systems constructed of terra-cotta pipe, culverts and flumes.

The Terra-Cotta Army was found a kilometer and a half east of the still-unexhumed mausoleum of the First Emperor, who was born in 259 BCE and ruled from 249 as the king of Qin. He became emperor in 221, holding that position until his death in 210. The emperor is credited with unifying China and expanding the building of the Great Wall. The extraordinary archaeological find was the emperor's retinue in death.

---

1 Tony Barnstone and Chou Ping, eds., *The Anchor Book of Chinese Poetry*. New York: Anchor Books 2005), 116.
2 See generally, http://usa.chinadaily.com.cn/life/2014-12/09/content_19053767.htm.

At the peak of construction, according to China's great historian of a century later, 700,000 workers labored on the emperor's mausoleum alone.³ One can only guess how many artists and artisans at the same time were shaping and sculpting the terra-cotta warriors and the rest of the retinue. Still only partially excavated, the Terra-Cotta Army has been aptly called the eighth wonder of the ancient world.⁴

---

3 始皇初即位，穿治郦山，及并天下，天下徒送诣七十余万人，穿三泉，下铜而致椁，宫观百官奇器珍怪徙臧满之。令匠作机弩矢，有所穿近者辄射之。以水银为百川 江河大海，机相灌输，上具天文，下具地理。以人鱼膏为烛，度不灭者久之。二世曰："先帝后宫非有子者，出焉不宜。皆令从死，死者甚众。葬既已下，或言工匠为机，臧皆知之，臧重即泄。大事毕，已臧，闭中羡，下外羡门，尽闭工匠臧者，无复出者。树草木以象山。["When the Emperor first came to the throne he began digging and shaping Mt. Li. Later, when he unified his empire, he had over 700,000 men from all over the empire transported to the spot. They dug down to the third layer of underground springs and poured in bronze to make the outer coffin. Replicas of palaces, scenic towers, and the hundred officials, as well as rare utensils and wonderful objects, were brought to fill up the tomb. Craftsmen were ordered to set up crossbows and arrows, rigged so they would immediately shoot down anyone attempting to break in. Mercury was used to fashion imitations of the hundred rivers, the Yellow River and the Yangtze, and the seas, constructed in such a way that they seemed to flow. Above were representations of all the heavenly bodies, below, the features of the earth. 'Man-fish' oil was used for lamps, which were calculated to burn for a long time without going out..."] 史记·秦始皇本纪, Sima Qian, *Shiji*, vol. 6, Burton Watson, tr., *Records of the Grand Historian* (Hong Kong: Columbia University Press, 1993), 63; another translation is found in Yang Hsien-yi and Gladys Yang, trs., *Selections from Records of the Historian* (Beijing: Foreign Languages Press, 1979), 186; and see Raymond Dawson, tr., *Sima Qian: The First Emperor* (Oxford: Oxford University Press, 2007), xi, xxiii.

4 See, e.g., Kinoshita, Hiromi (2007). Jane Portal. ed. *The First Emperor: China's Terracotta Army*. London: British Museum. ISBN 978-0-7141-2447-6; http://www.chinadaily.com.cn/china/2009-10/13/content_8786478.htm; http://www.dailymail.co.uk/news/article-480757/Curse-Terracotta-Army-How-discovered-relic-suffered-ruined-lives.html#ixzz1v6D15iSM;.

China in 1974 had not yet passed out of the dark period of its Cultural Revolution, which reigned like a tyrannical dynasty of old from 1966 until 1976, when Chairman Mao Zedong died. The reign of Mao, it happens, had much in common with the reign of the First Emperor. Upon the discovery of the Terra-Cotta Army the country's Ministry of Culture took control of the site, expelled the locals, including the farmers who had discovered it, and sent trained archaeologists to begin its disinterring.

Vagueness is the better part of discretion, which is better here than any valor. In the third year of the excavation, as pits two and three were worked, one of the Ministry's novice archaeologists, digging eight feet below ground, troweled, then brushed dirt from the figure of a scribe. The figure, made of the same terra cotta used for roof tiles and drainage pipes during the First Emperor's reign, was largely hollow inside. Some of the figures had proved fairly durable, but many were in fragments. In this case, the right leg had broken from its torso.

As the young archaeologist crouched in his pit, he found within the hollow torso two amber-colored cylinders. The amber was a casing, a hard, resin-like material, sealing something within it. Eager for glory, the archaeologist disregarded professional propriety (and party loyalty), and tried gently to bend one cylinder. Brittle, it crazed in a web of cracks, and the casing fell away.

What had been sealed within the amber casing was a silk scroll, supple and preserved in nearly pristine condition. The second amber cylinder, he could see, contained another scroll. Working out of sight of his colleagues, he unrolled the exposed scroll a few inches, enough to see vertical columns of Chinese characters, proceeding right to left, in the customary fashion. Based on the style of the calligraphy, he judged the documents to date from before the age of Sima Qian's *Shiji*. The *Shiji*, or *Historical Records*, is the seminal work (and prodigious — it consists of more than a half-million characters) of Chinese history. It was written in the century following the death of the First Emperor.

Such dating made sense. Someone, the archaeologist deduced, had secreted the scrolls in this terra-cotta figure about 213 BCE, perhaps as late as 210. For one thing, the project to create the figures had begun before 213, according to the Ministry's scholars, and continued until the emperor's death in 210. More important, in 213 the First Emperor had — according to Sima Qian, who represented the Han dynasty that had brought down the First Emperor's rule (history is written by the victors) — decreed the burning of all books in China. Sima Qian's history had been proven reliable in many instances, and, like most Chinese literati through the centuries, the archaeologist tended to take his account more or less as gospel. These scrolls were concealed within the terra-cotta figure, he believed without a doubt, to escape the Burning of the Books, as the event is known in Chinese history. To be concealed as they were, the scrolls must have contained writing considered especially precious by their hider, particularly odious to the emperor, or both.

If the writings would have offended the First Emperor, who knew who else their "seditious" content might offend? The First Emperor and the leaders of the Cultural Revolution shared one trait: they both persecuted intellectuals. The young archaeologist worried that the scrolls might be suppressed or, worse, destroyed. With that thought, he elected to conceal them from his colleagues and superiors. He swept together the shards of the amber casing, which was the thickness of thinnest glass, and later hid them away. With utmost circumspection he left the dig with the two scrolls that evening. Ultimately, he gave the scrolls to a friend at one of the scholarly institutes in China that study ancient Chinese manuscripts, so that they could be rendered into modern Chinese.[5]

---

5   The Zonghua Shuju in Beijing is perhaps the best known. It is not the institute in question.

Cangjie was historian to the Yellow Emperor forty-seven centuries ago, which is to say some two thousand five hundred years before the reign of the so-called *First* Emperor. At the behest of his master, the Yellow Emperor, Cangjie invented writing. That is the old story.

Much that is written of the Yellow Emperor is history, and much is legend. Much that is legend may be history. The Yellow Emperor united Han China. In doing so, he accomplished something neither Alexander nor Caesar nor Charlemagne nor Victoria would achieve: he conquered, gathered his conquests into empire, then forged his empire into a nation, one that survived not merely centuries but now nearly five thousand years. The story of the Yellow Emperor is this:

Huangdi, the future Yellow Emperor, around the year 2700 BCE defeated an army of a warring neighboring tribe.[6] Huangdi merged the two tribes, doubling his domain. Then a more warlike tribe threatened, led by Chi You and his eighty-one brothers, each having four eyes and eight arms. Each arm wielded a terrible weapon, and each brother held magical powers. Chi You himself had the power to exhale a fog that could shroud a battlefield. He could call down lightning on an enemy. Huangdi challenged those formidable powers nonetheless, riding a chariot of his invention that, sixteen centuries later, Hector or

---

6   Dates vary. The contemporary writer Ong Siew Chey writes that the Yellow Emperor's reign began in 2704 BCE and lasted one hundred years. *China Condensed: 5000 Years of History and Culture* (Marshall Cavendish International, 2008), 17. The *Columbia Encyclopedia* writes that his reign began in 2697, and gives no date for his death. http://www.encyclopedia.com/topic/Yellow_Emperor.aspx. Another authority writes that the Yellow Emperor reigned from 2696 until 2598 BCE: Herbert Allen Giles (1845–1935), *A Chinese Biographical Dictionary* (London: B. Quaritch, 1898), 338. Wikipedia gives the years of the Yellow Emperor's reign as either 2697–2597, or 2696–2596 BCE, citing various sources. https://en.wikipedia.org/wiki/Yellow_Emperor. I will arbitrarily accept the period 2697 to 2597; any roughly 100–year reign strains credulity.

Achilles would have coveted. He defeated Chiyou in an epic battle on the plains of Zhuolu. Dominion over the lands and people of Chiyou gave Huangdi dominion over all Han China. He became, by his decree, the Yellow Emperor.

The Yellow Emperor ruled, some say, for one hundred years, from 2697 until 2597 BCE. The bristlecone pine "Methuselah," long thought to be the oldest living thing on earth, which lives in anonymity in an eastern California forest, sprouted to a seedling the century after the Yellow Emperor's death. During the one hundred years of his reign, the Yellow Emperor divined the principles of traditional Chinese medicine, devised the Chinese calendar, and developed early forms of martial arts. His wife Leizu established sericulture; she taught women to spin thread from the cocoon filaments excreted by silkworms, and to weave cloth from the thread. His historian Cangjie invented writing.[7] In the medical, martial, and domestic arts, in astronomy and writing, Han Chinese civilization sprang up and flourished during the Yellow Emperor's reign.

Why did Cangjie invent writing? The emperor, it was said, wanted an effective means of delivering decrees to his subjects. And so he ordered Cangjie to devise such a means.[8] The American poet Billy Collins has written that Cangjie invented writing "after observing the tracks

---

[7] Today the system by which Chinese characters are entered into a computer by means of a standard keyboard is called the "Cangjie Method." It was invented in 1976 by Chu Bong-Foo. Its name was suggested by Chiang Wei-kuo, then Defence Minister of the Republic of China. http://en.wikipedia.org/wiki/Cangjie_input_method.

[8] See, e.g., https://en.wikipedia.org/wiki/Cangjie; http://www.chinaknowledge.de/History/Myth/personscangjie.html. Prior to the invention of writing many cultures used systems involving knotted strings or other markers. The use of knotted ropes, cords, or strings, found in many civilizations, was highly refined by the Incas. Their records were kept on such strings, called quipus (or khipus). See, e.g., "Untangling an Ancient Accounting Tool and a Stubborn Incan Mystery," *The New York Times*, Janury 3, 2016, 7.

of birds."[9] Another account has a phoenix dropping from his beak an odd hoof print that fell at Cangjie's feet, startling Cangjie with the inspiration he needed to fulfill the emperor's command. (Cangjie did not recognize the print; a hunter told him it was the print of a pixiu, a rare and strange animal.[10])

The Xian scrolls tell a different story. Written in the same hand, they tell us Cangjie had been a poet in the court of the Yellow Emperor (and likely something of a painter), and that he invented writing for a reason none of the stories tells. One, called the Beta Scroll, contains poems of a contemporary of the First Emperor, and is titled, roughly, "Dreams" or "Visions of Cangjie." I've chosen the latter title for this book. There is no mention of the writer's name, but he was not a bad poet, and more than a common laborer in the First Emperor's terra-cotta works. He was most likely a sculptor employed in the creation of the army, and the one responsible for hiding the scrolls in the figure.

The more important manuscript is the other, the Alpha Scroll. The sculptor, as I shall call him, tells us this scroll contains the actual poems of Cangjie that had been all but forgotten, had been omitted even from the fifth-century collection of Confucius, the *Shijing* (which was as much a collection of folk songs as anything), but that he, the sculptor, has rendered them into Classical Chinese (the written form of what we call Old Chinese).

The sculptor tells us he worked his renderings of Cangjie's poems largely from tortoise shell, ox scapulas, wood slats or ostraca — pieces of pottery or bits of bone — on which the poems had been carved or etched. The sculptor writes that Cangjie himself carved or etched the characters of his poems, though in difficult passages not yet fully trans-

---

9 Billy Collins, "Ornithography," *Ballistics* (2008), 83.
10 See, e.g., http://transenter.com/blog/chinese-characters/, and http://history.cultural-china.com/en/50History5684.html.

lated he seems to believe some of poems may have been transcribed from Cangjie's originals during the twenty-four centuries after Cangjie's death. The sculptor's renderings of Cangjie's poems here and there supply missing or indecipherable or untranslatable characters. These emendations, these "editorial liberties," are apparent — an anachorism here, an anachronism there. An example is the Buddha used as simile in an early poem of Cangjie. The historical Buddha did not walk the earth until two thousand years after the death of Cangjie, though he lived a few hundred years before the sculptor.

Conventional historical accounts have long maintained that the teachings of the Buddha did not reach China until the first century of the common era.[11] Were that true, the sculptor could not have known of the Buddha. Some recent scholarship, however, suggests that Buddhism may in fact have reached China by the third century BCE, contrary to the earlier thinking. The First Emperor, it is said, sought viciously to suppress the teachings of the Buddha, as he did most other learning.[12] The present texts lend support to the earlier date.

◐

I know of what I have just written, because I know something of Chinese history, and because I have read and translated substantial portions of the Xian Scrolls into English.

The scholar-friend to whom the archaeologist gave the scrolls has

---

11   Ong siew Chey, *China Condensed* (Singapore: Marshall Cavendish Editions, 2008), p. 103; http://www.britannica.com/biography/Mingdi.
12   At http://www.chinadaily.com.cn/life/2009-05/13/content_7772181.htm, Han Wei, a noted researcher with the Shaanxi Provincial Institute of Archeology, is quoted as saying, "China's first and most influential history book, *The Historical Records*, stated clearly that Emperor Qin Shihuang (259–210 BC) strictly banned Buddhism and Buddhist temples."

been a colleague and friend of mine for three decades. Eight years ago we met at a conference in a provincial capital in China. To be prudent, I should not give the name of the city, or province. In a teahouse he told me the story of the scrolls, explaining he had not dared write me about them, and had worriedly stored them for some thirty years. He suspected they were authentic, but was wary of putting in the time necessary to study them properly in China. He wanted to know if he could entrust the serious work of study and translation to me. A few days later, after perusing one of the scrolls in private, the scroll I have called "Beta," I agreed. With the aid of a friend at one of my country's consulates in China, I had the scrolls sent by diplomatic pouch to my country's foreign ministry, and from there delivered to me. I had them photographed twice by museum archival technicians. I worked from one set of photographs, secured the second set in a safe place, and hid the scrolls themselves even more securely in a safe-deposit box. When I and my scholar-friend have died, testamentary letters will reveal the location of the scrolls. The young archaeologist passed away a year ago in mysterious circumstances, and we suspect his theft had been discovered; this is the reason for our circumspection.

The Xian Scrolls are written in Classical Chinese, the written form of the language common during the early and middle Zhou Dynasty (1122 BCE–256 BCE), and somewhat later. The *Shijing* of Confucius, for example, and the *Shiji* (Sima Qian's *Historical Records),* are written in this language. Middle Chinese, by contrast, was used during the dynasties that reigned, roughly, between the sixth and tenth centuries CE. It is the language of the poetry of Li Bai (sometimes known in English as Li Po, following a Victorian system of transliteration) and Du Fu (Tu Fu).

I am not Chinese, nor am I resident in China, though I have studied there. I am not Raymond Dawson, the scholar who has translated portions of the 130 scrolls of the *Historical Records*,[13] although we do have certain learning in common. Middle Chinese is my forte; I am less proficient in Old Chinese. When reading, and especially when translating Old Chinese into English, I often seek the advice of colleagues more knowledgeable than me. For this work I have been able to call on them when confronted with a character unfamiliar to me, or a character having illegible portions, because of a rend or tear, or mere fading. ("Have you an idea what this character would have looked like were the manuscript intact?") I made perhaps fifty such inquiries, and only twice did my correspondent have the curiosity to ask what I was working on. Perhaps my scholar friends were merely being polite. Each time a simple, "A quaint scroll I came across," sufficed as an answer.

The poems in this book are the first translations of the Xian Scrolls. They are English translations of some of the shorter poems of Cangjie, dating from about 2650 BCE, and of the sculptor, Cangjie's transcriber, written about 213 BCE. They await more worthy translations, such as the vibrant (though insufficiently informed) translations of the *Shijing* by Ezra Pound, which seemed so fresh following the stuffy Victorian translations that preceded it.[14]

Cangjie's writings, revealed here as the oldest known Chinese poems, are perhaps the oldest known poems on earth. They are older even than the poems, or hymns, of Enheduanna, the daughter of King Sargon of Akkad, who is often described as the first-named literary author in history.[15] Enheduanna's short life spanned the years 2285–2250 BCE. The better-known Epic of Gilgamesh dates from a century or two later than Enheduanna's haunting, and enormously influential verses.[16] Akkad was in northwest Mesopotamia, the land "between the rivers," between, that

---

13 *Sima Qian, The First Emperor*, published by Oxford University Press, most recently in 2007.
14 For a scholarly look at Pound's translations, see http://surface.syr.edu/eng_etd/28/.
15 Http://www.penn.museum/blog/museum/ur-digitization-project-item-of-the-month-june-2012/; for renderings of several of her hymns, or poems, see http://classicalarthistory.weebly.com/1/post/2012/04/enheduanna-poems.html.
16 The oldest of the poems of the Epic of Gilgamesh is thought to date to the Third Dynasty of Ur, roughly 2150-2000 BCE. See, e.g., http://www.class.uidaho.edu/engl257/ancient/epic_of_gilgamesh.htm.

is, the Tigris and Euphrates Rivers. Sargon had conquered all of that fertile "cradle of civilization," meaning, of course, Western civilization. In Western civilization's other cradle, the Nile River Valley, the oldest known poem we have is "The Tale of the Shipwrecked Sailor," which is younger yet, dating from the twentieth century BCE.[17] Likewise, the oldest extant South Asian texts, the Sanskrit Vedas, date only from the early second millennium BCE.

◐

China's is one of the world's oldest living cultures. One scholar has written that "for the Chinese, the essence of civilization was the art of writing."[18] And poetry has historically held the highest rank in Chinese civilization. Professor J. P. Seaton describes poetry's "extremely elevated place…" in Chinese civilization. "In traditional Chinese culture," he writes, "poetry occupied a station unrivaled by any other single talent, ability, or practical accomplishment as a source of prestige, affluence, and even political power."[19]

The poems of Cangjie are older, considerably older, than what were previously thought to be the oldest Chinese poems, older even than the poem long said, however implausibly, to be the first Chinese poem.[20] Cangjie's poems, crystalline in image at times, slant in emotion at others, and foreshadowing five thousand years to come of Chinese poetry, might find in time, with proper translation, a place in the higher history of poetry.

The Xian scrolls, containing as they do glimpses of Chinese history

---

17   John L. Foster, tr., *Ancient Egyptian Literature: An Anthology* (Austin: University of Texas Press, 2012), 8–16.
18   Margaret Oliphant, *The Atlas of the Ancient World* (New York: Barnes & Noble 1992), 162.
19   J. P. Seaton, tr. and ed., *The Shambhala Anthology of Chinese Poetry* (Boston and London: Shambhala, 2006), xi–xii.
20   "The Peasant's Song" is that poem, and both Mencius and Chuang Tzu described it as the first Chinese poem. See n. 25.

(not to mention a touching, though to a modern reader perhaps a simple poetry), have a capacity to awe. Even more so when we reflect that as the sculptor was doing his work, most books in China were being burned. These works confirm Sima Qian's story, for the sculptor writes plaintively of the Burning of the Books. That is how we know that he was working in 213 BCE, or shortly afterward; the First Emperor died in 210.

In 221 BCE the First Emperor, Qin Huangdi ("Huangdi" means emperor; before becoming emperor his name was Qin Shihuang), had by serial conquests reassembled and enlarged the empire that the Yellow Emperor had put together almost twenty-five hundred years before, which in the interval had disintegrated into a large number of perpetually warring states. His dynasty was called the Qin, after his own name— "Qin" is pronounced "Chin," and it gives us the current country name, "China." To exalt himself above the divinity and veneration of the Yellow Emperor, he issued a series of decrees to secure his station. One of the first such decrees proclaimed himself the *First* Emperor (so as to distinguish himself from the Yellow Emperor). Another decree, issued eight years later in 213 BCE, ordered the Burning of the Books.

For this period in Chinese history, two and a half millennia after the time of the Yellow Emperor and Cangjie, we have a solid historian. (Cangjie, for all we know, may himself have been an equally sound historian of the period of the Yellow Emperor. But whatever he may have written of the history of that era, had it survived until the Burning of the Books, was most likely destroyed in 213.) Sima Qian, who was born in 145 BCE and became Grand Historiographer in 100 BCE, wrote the *Historical Records* the century after the First Emperor's death. Writing as an enemy of the Qin, he gives us the text of the chilling proposal that became the decree for the Burning of the Books:

> Your servant requests that the records of the historians apart from those of Qin should all be burnt. Apart from those copies which the scholars of broad learning are responsible for in their

official capacity, anyone in all under Heaven who dares to possess and hide away the *Songs* [the *Shi Jing*, collected by Confucius], the *Documents*, and the sayings of the hundred schools, should hand them all over to a governor or commandant and they should be indiscriminately burnt. If there is anyone who dares to mention the *Songs* or *Documents* in private conversation, he should be executed. Those who, using the old, reject the new will be wiped out together with their clans.... There should be exemption for books concerned with medicine, pharmacy, divination by tortoiseshell and milfoil, the sowing of crops, and the planting of trees....[21]

In his endeavor to destroy writing, the First Emperor succeeded to a degree rarely equaled, much less exceeded, by other tyrants of history who have also sought to destroy the written record, and thereby the cultural soul of their enemies, or subjects.[22] Nearly all Chinese writing — legal, literary, historical, or religious — was burned. Only a few writings were to be preserved — those kept in the First Emperor's palaces. Those were for the exclusive use of the Emperor and his scholars, so Sima Qian tells us.

According to a present-day scholar, the purpose of the Burning of the Books was not so much "to exterminate learning, but to monopolize

---

[21] Raymond Dawson, tr. and ed., *Sima Qian, The First Emperor: Selections from the Historical Records* (Oxford: Oxford University Press 2007) 74–75, vii–viii, xxxix.

[22] The Nazis burned Jewish texts in the 1930s, as had the French crown in 1242, which ordered the burning of 12,000 copies of the Talmud. In the early sixteenth century the Spanish bishop Diego de Landa ordered the burning of the entire literature of the Maya, thinking it Satanic. Only four books are known to have survived that auto-da-fe. During World War II conquering Japanese military units burned numerous libraries in China. See generally http://en.wikipedia.org/wiki/List_of_book-burning_incidents.

it by ensuring that copies were available only to academicians working in the imperial library."[23] Soon though, rebellions against the First Emperor produced burnings of their own — fires that raged for three months, destroying the emperor's palaces and in them the few copies of literature that had been preserved for the use of the emperor, and his personal scholars.[24]

Before the discovery of the Xian Scrolls, the oldest-known Chinese poetry consisted of three collections and one small poem long thought to be the oldest Chinese poem. These collections, and the one small poem, had miraculously survived the Burning of the Books. The small poem, the one thought until now to be the oldest Chinese poem, is "The Peasant's Song.:[25]

"The Peasant's Song," J. P. Seaton writes, is "rough-voiced," and perhaps it is,[26] but it is pure voiced, and sings themes expressed by later poets such as the greatest of Chinese poets, Li Bai (Li Po; 701–762 CE),

---

23 Dawson, 149.
24 Dawson, 119, 157.
25 Of those three collections, the first is the *Shi Jing* (Classics of Poetry) of Confucius, which in tradition dates from the Spring and Autumn Period, roughly 722 to 481 BCE (though historians disagree). The second collection is the *Daode jing*, the seminal work of Daoism which, according to legend, was written by Laozi in the fourth and third centuries BCE, though historians are by no means sure there was a Laozi. See, e.g., Barnstone and Ping, *The Anchor Book of Chinese Poetry* (New York: Anchor Books 2005, pp. 12-13). The third collection is the *Chu Ci* (Songs of Chu), written during the Warring States Period, 476 to 221 BCE. While the Shijing is a collection of poems from the northern, Yellow River region of China, the later Chu Ci is a collection from the Yangtse River region to the south.

"The Peasant's Song," until now the poem thought to be the oldest known Chinese poem, has been described as well as the first Chinese poem, by both Mencius (a founder of Confucianism) and by Chuang Tzu (founder of Taoism). J. P. Seaton, translator and editor, *The Shambhala Anthology of Chinese Poetry* (Boston and London: Shambhala, 2006), xxi.

26 Seaton, xxi, 3.

the "banished immortal."²⁷ Some, to be sure, assert that Du Fu (Tu Fu; 712–770) was the greatest of Chinese poets. In an extraordinary coincidence of history, Li Bai and Du Fu were contemporaries, and dear friends.²⁸ In the much older verses of Cangjie, we find themes of "The Peasant's Song" expressed with more subtlety, more imagination. Here is "The Peasant's Song":

The Peasant's Song

Sunups we work,
Sundowns we rest.
Dig wells, we drink,
Plow fields, we eat.
What has an emperor
To do with us?²⁹

The poem opens as the plainest imaginable description of the daily lives of peasants living in any countryside in any part of the earth then. But it ends with a coda of sublime indifference, blithe contempt even, for the "emperor" — or, to be precise, an even less important "*an* emperor."

A number of the verses of Cangjie speak (not at all with affection)

---

27 Li Bai, "by almost unanimous consent, is regarded as the greatest poet under the Tangs, and of China of all times." Obata, 2. (Maddeningly, Li Bai's name is rendered into English in too many ways — Li Pai, Li T'ai-po, Li T-ai-pai, and the Wade-Giles transliteration, Li Po. "Li Bai is probably the best-known Chinese poet in the West. He and Du Fu (Tu Fu) are considered the finest poets of the Tang dynasty. *The Anchor Book of Chinese Poetry*, 116. William Hung considered Du Fu China's great poet; his book title (see next note) tells that much.

28 William Hung, *Tu Fu: China's Greatest Poet* (Cambridge: Harvard University Press, 1952); David Hinton, tr. and ed., *The Selected Poems of Tu Fu* (New York: New Directions, 1989), vii–x.

29 After Seaton, 11.

of an emperor, the Yellow Emperor. Verses of the sculptor, the transcriber of Cangjie's poems, also speak occasionally of an emperor, the First Emperor. At times Cangjie's emperor seems a conjured emperor, at times not. The loathed emperor of the sculptor, though, is not a conjured emperor, no mere metaphor for life's oppressions and petty oppressors. He is, plainly, the historical figure the First Emperor, the Burner of the Books.

The moon figures prominently in early Chinese poetry, and that is especially true of Cangjie's poems. Many of the *Shijing* poems, those collected by Confucius in the fifth century BCE, sing of the moon. (The 305 poems in this collection have been variously dated from 1046 to 700 BCE, and from the eighth to fifth centuries BCE. "The Peasant's Song" is thought only to be older than the oldest ode of the *Shijing*.) Ode 143, for example, begins (in Ezra Pound's translation), "The erudite moon is up, less fair than she/who hath tied silk cords about/a heart in agony . . . ." Ode 193, which deals in part with a solar eclipse (August 29, 776 BCE), includes the lines "Moon gnawed out, sun under yoke,/ Pity the folk beneath./ Sun, moon, foretell evil?"[30] Even practical Confucius, it seems, may have occasionally been enchanted by the White Goddess, the moon. (The moon later figures as well in many of the poems of Li Bai, who lived and wrote in the eighth century CE.[31])

The moon as an image — or as not — occurs and recurs in Cangjie's poems. One difficulty in translating Cangjie is that there is no Chinese poetry contemporary with his for comparison. But then we are not translating Cangjie's words of nearly five thousand years ago; we are

---

30 These translations are from Ezra Pound, *Shi-ching: The Classic Anthology Defined by Confucius* (Cambridge, MA: Harvard University Press, 1982), 69, 107.

31 William Hung, *Tu Fu: China's Greatest Poet* (Cambridge: Harvard University Press, 1952); David Hinton, tr. and ed., *The Selected Poems of Tu Fu* (New York: New Directions, 1989), vii–x.

translating translations of his words done 2200 years ago. And so, the translational issues are more than usually formidable, and fraught with conundrums. Was "moon" a word for soul in Cangjie's time, as a word for breath has been one in ours? If so, did the sculptor, his translator, know that when he used the word?

Here is an early poem from the *Shijing* (the same Ode 143, but in a translation different from Pound's), which echoes verses of the much earlier Cangjie. (Note that in its first stanza, the "white rising moon" is not *like* the beauty of the beloved; it *is* her beauty, perhaps her soul.)

White Moonrise

The white rising moon
Is your bright beauty
Binding me in spells
Till my heart's devoured.

The light moon soars
Resplendent like my lady,
Binding me in light chains
Till my heart's devoured.

Moon in white glory,
You are the beautiful one
Who delicately wounds me
Till my heart's devoured.[32]

---

32 From a translation by Tony Barnstone and Willis Barnstone, *The Anchor Book of Chinese Poetry*, 7. This is Ode 143, and the translation is a far cry from Ezra Pound's.

If the "moon" of the *Shijing,* or of Cangjie, can mean beauty, or soul, when should it be rendered "moon" in English, and when not?

Cangjie tells us he was not the first poet. He writes with longing of the forgotten poems of a great poet, Li Won. Li Won in turn, Cangjie tells, had sung of the first poet.

The poems of Cangjie seem at times scenes from a pastoral Constable Country poetry. The familiarity can disturb, though, as when a lover in a dream slowly shows to be a long-dead mother, when dawn drowns in deeper night, when a child's eyes seem at once those of an animal. Is this a description of a glance within, a glimpse of another world, of an afterlife? —

> the unending violet horizon
> and ever rising moon....

The French Symbolist poet Stéphane Mallarmé famously remarked, "All poetry has gone wrong since the great Homeric deviation." What would Mallarmé have said of this poetry, composed two thousand years before his Homer veered?

☽

Five thousand years almost have passed since the time of the Yellow Emperor and his historian, the inventor of writing, the poet Cangjie. For twenty-five hundred years Cangjie's poems had been preserved, barely, and they were nearly lost when in 213 BCE the First Emperor set out to burn all books in China. Miraculously the poems of Cangjie were preserved in translations of the Chinese of that day.

Twenty-two hundred years have passed since then. Old Chinese, the Chinese of the era of the First Emperor, is in respects more different from modern Chinese than Old English is from modern English. That is to say that the words of the sculptor, the transcriber of the poems of Cangjie at the time of the Burning of the Books, are more foreign to a reader of modern Chinese than the words of *Beowulf* are to a reader of modern English. That should not surprise. The Old English of *Beowulf*, the great English epic poem, dates anywhere from the eighth century CE to as late as the eleventh century. Put another way, the earliest *Beowulf* could have been written was the century Li Bai was writing his timeless lyrics in Chinese. Li Bai seems so very "modern" when read beside the tales of Grendel, the Geats, and the denizens of the mead-hall Heorot that slog and slither through *Beowulf*. The translations of the finder of Cangjie's poems were written, at the least, a thousand years earlier than those dark dense words of *Beowulf*. Cangjie's poems were written two and a half millennia before that.

The sculptor, the transcriber of Cangjie's poems, may have found the Chinese of Cangjie to be at least equally different, and difficult, as a reader of modern Chinese finds the Old Chinese of the sculptor. After all, an even longer time had elapsed between Cangjie's time and the sculptor's, than has elapsed between the sculptor's time and today. The sculptor, a poet in his own right, never tells us though, of struggles with transcription, or translation. Had written Chinese evolved but little in those 2500 years? Was the sculptor privy to some secret knowledge of the Chinese of the time of Cangjie? Or was he a myth-maker too?

E. O.
London, February 12, 2016

The Lost Poems of Cangjie was published by Risk Press, 2016, under the oversight of Charlie Pendergast, in collaboration with Saint Mary's College of California, Moraga. The text was prepared by John Briscoe and edited, designed, and typeset in Garamond Premier Pro by Thomas Christensen. The cover image was generously provided by the artist, Hung Liu. Books were printed and sewn bound in China on 180 gsm creamy woodfree paper by Global PSD.